Sip Tea with Mad Hatter
at KAMP®

Kids Arts & Manners Program
*The Golden Rule Applies

LORETTA NEFF
FOUNDER, EW FOUNDATION
ILLUSTRATED BY ANIRBAN MITRA

Neff Publishing, LLC.
401 S. County Rd.
PO Box 3303
Palm Beach, FL 33480
Tel: (561) 833-0131
www.EWBooks.org

Ordering Information

Individual or quantity sales. Special discounts are available on quantity purchases by corporations, associations, and others. Our books are available through most bookstores. They can also be ordered directly from www.EWBooks.org or by calling (561)833-0131.

Printed in China

This book is printed on acid-free paper

Published by Neff Publishing, LLC

ISBN: 978-0-9985559-0-4

Library of Congress Control Number: 2016921613

Contents

Appendix

Introduction: A Note to Parents, Caregivers, and Teachers

With our demanding modern schedules, it's all too easy to overlook introducing important social skills to our children. Learning basic etiquette and manners early, especially during childhood, can shape a child's character and greatly impact his or her life for the better.

The EW Foundation's (EWF) vision is to teach, inspire, and motivate children to perform spontaneous acts of kindness and consideration. The benefits they receive from simple, good behavior will be both tangible and intangible. Our belief is that children can "do well by doing good deeds."

The topics covered in this book are part of the EW Foundation's award-winning KAMP® curriculum, a 2015 and 2016 *Promising Practices* national award winner by Washington, DC-based *Character.org*.

Sip Tea with Mad Hatter makes learning afternoon tea manners fun, meaningful, and most important, memorable. Any adult or child who reads this book will delight in the clever illustrations and correlations of *Alice in Wonderland*'s characters to the manners advice.

Phrases like "Be as cool as a Cheshire cat," "Don't be a mean Red Queen," and "My teacup runneth over with gratitude" are easy-to-grasp concepts for children.

You're invited:
A Mad Hat·terrific Afternoon Tea

Please join me for an afternoon tea and unbirthday party! Together we can dive down the rabbit hole with Alice, meet Mad Hatter and friends, and be amazed by the magical sights and sounds of an unbirthday celebration in Wonderland. Whose unbirthday, you ask? Why, in Wonderland it's everyone's unbirthday 364 days of the year!

But before we dive into all the fun, there are a few wonder-rules we should learn that will add to the enjoyment of others—our fellow tea party guests—and ours and keep us happy and safe during our celebration. A grand adventure and knowledge await us!

Come Drive Us Mad and Give Your Parents and Teachers a Break!

Winsome Behavior and Wonder-rules of the Land (Weird, Quirky Traits are Welcome!)

- Seek knowledge through reading and follow the rules in order to have fun and stay safe.
- Stand tall—even if you're small!—and introduce yourself with confidence and courage.
- Use your best tea manners with dignity and flair to honor special guests.
- Be a magnificent host by showing curiosity and integrity.
- Be a delightful dream guest—not a daydreaming one—by showing compassion and determination.
- For birthday parties and celebrations, display "cool" behavior and show the spirit of giving and receiving gifts with enthusiasm and humility.
- Be resilient, treat others with respect, and show respect for yourself.
- Be kind and patient—never mean.
- Show creativity and gratitude with a signature work of art.
- Put your best foot forward with a basic box step or be hip and do a freestyle futterwacken dance.

I. Absolem: Knowledge and Obedience

Read books to reach new heights!

Absolem is a clever caterpillar who absolutely loves to read. It's how he spends most of his free time. He knows that books can feed his imagination and take him anywhere he wants to go. He also knows the more he reads, the more he develops, learns, and is able to share with others—and the sooner he'll become a butterfly. In Wonderland, Absolem can always be found sharing "Bubbles of Wisdom" with others. He is masterful at teaching others the rules of the land. He tells us just enough rules to keep everyone safe and still have lots of fun.

Absolem fills the air with "Bubbles of Wisdom" and encourages others to read and learn in order to become the very best they can be. He explains, "Life is filled with choices, and knowledge will help you make the best ones."

When receiving an invitation, reading it carefully will help you enjoy the event. Read any instructions, make a note of the date, dress for the occasion, and be on time.

At celebrations and parties, your behavior will decide how you'll be remembered. Absolem hopes you'll always make wise decisions and be remembered as a dream guest, not as a guest who spoiled the dream.

Follow the rules and fun will follow!

- Arrive and leave on time to show respect for your host.
- Dress for the occasion.
- Follow the host's rules.

II. Alice: Confidence and Courage

Stand tall like Alice and greet with confidence!

Alice is sugar and spice and everything nice, and she's also quite adventurous. She knows that meeting new people and introducing yourself requires enormous courage. It's well worth giving it your best try, because meeting new people can be exciting and rewarding. As Alice stumbles upon different and sometimes frightening people in the forest, such as Mad Hatter and his friends, she stands tall—even though she's small—smiles, and says her first and last name: "Hello, I'm Alice Kingsleigh."

Greetings are easy when you see people you know, like a classmate from school, neighbor, or your grandparents. When meeting new people for the first time, though, it's normal to feel a little bit awkward. The best way to overcome this feeling is by repetition. With some practice, you can be as self-assured as Alice when meeting new people. Are you excited to meet new friends in Wonderland?

Introduce yourself with confidence!

- Stand tall—even if you're small!—and show courage and confidence.
- Smile! Smiling at someone always makes him or her want to smile back at you in return. It's contagious, just like laughing!
- Make direct eye contact to show interest and sincerity.
- Say your first and last name.

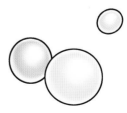

III. Mad Hatter and Friends: Dignity and Honor

Royal Table Manners for an Afternoon Tea

Mad Hatter, as host, rolls out the royal tea treatment.

Teas are a wonderful way to spend time with friends and frolic in the afternoon. Having excellent table manners doesn't mean you can't still have fun—it just means that when you eat with others, you should think about your actions.

For example, if you were to talk with food in your mouth, wipe a runny nose on your napkin, or sneeze without turning away from the table, you could pass germs around or disgust another guest. Also, as tempting as it may be to use your spoon like a catapult to send sugar cubes into the air, you could break something or hurt someone. The same is true for going completely bonkers and jumping on furniture or throwing plates like Frisbees. Both of those things are not only dangerous, but frowned upon by adults. In fact, breaking plates could cost you privileges. There are safer and less costly ways to have fun!

Let's have excellent table manners as we greet our host and tea party friends!

- Tiptoe through Wonderland on your way to the table—don't run as if you are part of the Red Queen's army!
- Remember that Alice and Mad Hatter, as guest of honor and host, sit at the heads of the table.
- Put your napkin on your lap immediately after you are seated.
- Use extra care with fragile china plates and saucers.

Tasty tea sandwiches and desserts to treasure!

A children's tea menu often includes a specialty tea flavor, such as raspberry or strawberry, as well as hot chocolate with marshmallows. Snacks are often finger-sized sandwiches of peanut butter and jelly, grilled cheese, chopped egg salad, and chicken salad. Eye-catching miniature cakes, cookies, and warm scones served with jam and cream usually follow. Yum! The items you'll be offered are usually listed on a special menu designed just to accompany the tea, to help you identify each choice:

If you touch it, you must take it!

- To keep from spreading germs, take any item you touch in a buffet line or when sharing items from a serving bowl or plate.
- Use a clean piece of silverware to scoop dipping sauces or jams onto your plate.
- Tear your scone into two parts before applying butter, preserves, or clotted cream.
- You may use your fingers to pick up celery sticks, cucumbers, raw carrots, and other finger foods. You may also use serving tongs if provided.

Sip your beverage, don't slurp!

- Bring your cup or glass and food to your mouth; don't bring your face to your food by hunching over the table.
- Chew your food with your mouth closed.
- Finish chewing and swallowing before talking or taking a drink.
- Pat your mouth with your napkin—don't wipe. Be careful not to place the soiled part of the napkin on your pants or dress.
- Excuse yourself from the seating area or table if you need to use the restroom or blow your nose.
- Place your napkin on your chair or to the left of your plate when you leave the table during a meal—both ways are correct.
- When you are finished eating, place your silverware on a slant at the four o'clock position.
- Place your napkin to the left of your place setting when you're finished eating.

Be a Magnificent Host with Muchness

Show curiosity and integrity!

Mad Hatter is a magnificent host with muchness! Yes, muchness! In Wonderland, that word refers to a person who has passion and a very big heart. A host with muchness cares about his guests' comfort and wants everyone to have a memorable time.

A host with muchness also shows curiosity by asking his or her guests fun and interesting questions. And he listens carefully to the answers.

"Do you take sugar with your tea?
Do you fancy my hat?
Do you have the time?
Have you any allergies?
What makes honey so sweet?
Have you any idea why a raven is like a writing desk?"

A host with muchness shows integrity by honoring his word, telling the truth, and owning his mistakes—not blaming others.

Mad Hatter is thoughtful and includes every guest in the conversation and in games. He walks guests to the door when the party is over and says, "I had a fabulous time! I'm so glad you were a part of it!"

What makes Mad Hatter so magnificent is his madness, but in a very good way! Mad Hatter is "mad"—crazy—about having a frolicking fun time with friends. Ask yourself, "Is anyone crazy for wanting to have fun with friends?" Well of course not! That would be silly—all kids want to have fun!

Show guests a frolicking good time!

- Ask questions, even silly ones, and listen to the answers.
- Play games that can include every guest.
- Honor your word and tell the truth.
- Take responsibility for your mistakes.
- Walk guests to the door when the party's over and thank them for coming.

IV. Dormouse: Compassion and Determination

Be a Delightful Dream Guest—Not a Daydreamy One

The Golden Rule rules!

By all accounts, Dormouse is a delightful mouse who has a way of making others feel special. Dormouse understands that a guest's behavior can bring delight or, in some cases, disaster. Each guest plays an important role in putting the "dream" into a "dream celebration." Dormouse is always determined to be a dream guest himself.

However, Dormouse has personality flaws just like the rest of us. One of his challenges is to stay awake at a party. But when he is awake, he dazzles with his stories! He's even been known to draw a crowd.

Dormouse shares, "*The best way to make and keep friends is to always treat animals and people as you would like to be treated.*"

Dormouse always ends story time on a high note. For example, he'll place his book on a tea tray and pick up a cookie, then pause for dramatic effect. He'll look at his captive audience, remove his glasses, and close with, "I believe friends are a lot like cookies. Having different kinds are what makes life so sweet and yummy. Sure, you may have a favorite, but if you never try any others, you may never know what you're missing!" Then he'll giggle as he slides down from his mushroom and takes a bow.

No story time would be complete without a sing-along with the Alice in Wonderland Symphony Chorus! Mad Hatter knows this is just the thing to keep his guest, Dormouse, interested in what's going on at the party so he won't fall asleep again.

Do Your Best to Be a Dream Guest!

- Tell fun and positive stories—do not gossip or tell lies.
- Invite everyone to eat, play, and sing along. Do not pick favorites.
- Honor one another's differences and unique traits.
- Keep the conversation moving by asking other guests interesting questions.
- Participate in whatever activities the host has planned.

♪ Up above ♪♪
♪ the world you fly,
like a tea tray
in the sky. ♪
♪♪ Twinkle, twinkle . . .

VI. Cheshire Cat: Enthusiasm and Humility

The Spirit of Giving and Receiving

Be enthusiastic but humble, and always exhibit the "cool" behavior of Cheshire Cat.

Cheshire Cat is not an "aristocat," nor does he care to try to be. He's a "cool cat" with plenty of self-confidence, and is truly happy and comfortable in his own skin—even though it has been threatened by the Red Queen in more than one way! Cheshire Cat knows that he can be "cool" and humble at the same time. A "cool cat" also knows to purr to show subtle enthusiasm when experiencing pleasures, not to brag or boast.

Cheshire Cat purrs while chasing Dormouse, climbing up trees, meandering through alleys, playing with balls of yarn, and blowing bubbles at the welcome reception.

Cheshire Cat also knows that when cake and presents arrive, it's hard to hold back your excitement. So as a reminder, think of him walking right up in front of you and flashing his big, mysterious grin—reminding you to keep "cool." You must "grin and bear" your impatience a little longer.

Whether you are giving or receiving a gift, always be cool and try to act humbly like Cheshire Cat.

Be humble when giving or receiving gifts!

- Be gracious; show the same amount of enthusiasm for all the gifts you receive so that no one has his or her feelings hurt.
- Purr with pleasure—do not brag or boast about a gift you're giving or receiving. Never talk about how much a gift costs.
- Say "thank you" and show joy with your facial expression and behavior, even if the gift isn't what you hoped you would get.
- Sharing a gift that can be shared, such as a game or food, is a good deed.

VII. The Red Queen of Hearts: Kindness and Patience

Be kind and patient. Don't be a mean Red Queen!

The Red Queen is wicked and mean and everything in between. She wants everything her way and doesn't like to wait for anything! It's not possible to always get what you want exactly when you want it every day. Learning patience will keep you from becoming disappointed by this fact. Others will admire you for remaining calm in difficult situations, and you will be a good role model to younger children too.

Your parents are right when they say, "Patience is a virtue." It's a good thing. You don't want to act like a mean Red Queen and throw temper tantrums. If you do, you risk losing your head—literally! So, take your manners with you wherever you go and don't give the mean Red Queen a chance to say, "Off with your head!"

Red Queen was a big bully. Do you know what happens to bullies? Eventually they get what they deserve. Remember what happened to the Red Queen after Alice slayed the Jabberwocky dragon? She was exiled from Wonderland and forbidden to return. People with good hearts don't bully other people, nor would they allow someone to be bullied.

Don't lose your head—practice patience!

- Wait patiently in buffet lines or to be served—no fussing, complaining, or cutting.
- Be conscious not to disturb other guests or diners; talk or giggle quietly in public places.
- Be kind. Do not name-call, tease others, or use any kind of roughness.
- Tell an adult if you know about or see someone being bullied.

VIII. Tweedledee and Tweedledum: Resilience and Respect

Learning Resilience and Having Respect for Others and Yourself

Resilience and Respect Are Rules of Thumb for Tweedledee and Tweedledum!

Tweedledee and Tweedledum are the best of chums. They walk to the beat of their own drum, but together they enjoy friends, play games, and share adventures in Wonderland.

On occasion, Tweedledee and Tweedledum have been picked on for having unusual names, the way they talk, and even the way they dress. But they understand only people who are scared and insecure poke fun at others. They learned not to worry about what others think and to be resilient. They ignore hurtful comments.

Teasing in fun is a bit different. Tweedledee and Tweedledum love the game of croquet and are very competitive—they may tease each other during the game, for example, but never allow the joking to take on a hurtful tone. They always treat each other with respect.

Showing respect to someone else means you act in a way that shows you care about his or her feelings. This means you treat people with courtesy and politeness, act friendly, and don't call people mean names. Showing good manners toward others also shows that you respect yourself and them too.

Respect should be shown wherever you are: at home or school; on the playground or school bus; or in public places like an auditorium, club, gymnasium, hotel, or theater.

Be resilient and bounce back with a bright attitude!

Keeping a bright, cheery attitude; being considerate of others; and using magic words such as please, thank you, you're welcome, excuse me, and I'm sorry will keep memorable moments happy. Use them often, and you will do well throughout your whole life—and you'll enjoy the adventures of Wonderland!

It is important to show respect for someone by respecting his or her space and things.

- Be polite—don't snoop or ask personal or nosy questions.
- Respect your surroundings. Do not damage game pieces, touch displays or banners, or put your feet on top of chairs or tables.
- Throw any paper, plastic wrappers, or cups into a trash container—not on the floor.

IX. March Hare: Creativity and Gratitude

Think Outside the Rabbit Hole to Express Thanks

A creative guest would never forget to show gratitude and thank his or her host!

March Hare is a creative little rabbit with a huge imagination. He treasures teatime and is grateful to have friends with whom to share tea. His pocket watch lets him know when it's teatime. His large ears enable him to communicate with and listen to his fellow guests. But even more than he loves teatime, March Hare loves to draw and doodle. He could just drift away and draw for hours.

With his creative eye and keen memory, March Hare never forgets to show gratitude. He is known for handcrafting works of art and loves knowing that a one-of-a-kind creation he gives someone could become a keepsake.

Be creative and show gratitude by making a signature work of art as a thank-you note!

- Make one when something thoughtful has been done for you.
- Make one when you have received a gift.
- Make one just because you feel like letting someone know they are a special person in your life.

X. Graceful White Queen: Flexibility and Grace

"Tea" Dance Lesson

No one in Wonderland dances more gracefully than the White Queen!

The White Queen's graceful movements resemble the elegant dance movements of a fox-trot or waltz. In fact, she dances more gracefully than anyone else in Wonderland.

Create a 12-by-12-inch square for kids (or an 18-by-18-inch square for young adults) on the floor with masking tape and softly repeat the rhythm, "Slow, quick, quick, slow" as you take your steps. "Fly Me to the Moon" and "Moon River" are songs with perfect beats for practicing these steps. Once you've mastered the box step, you can apply what you've learned to other music as well. For fun, try dancing to Pharell Williams's "Happy" song or Justin Timberlake's "Can't Stop The Feeling."

The Box Step—Fox-Trot

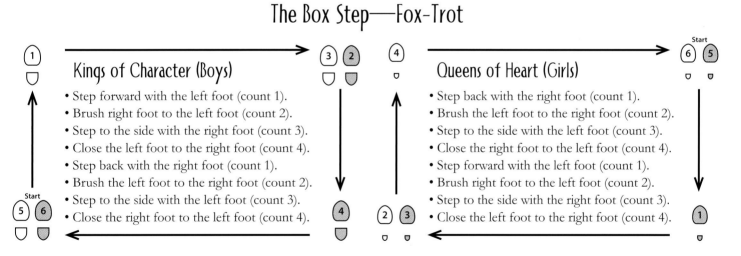

Kings of Character (Boys)
- Step forward with the left foot (count 1).
- Brush right foot to the left foot (count 2).
- Step to the side with the right foot (count 3).
- Close the left foot to the right foot (count 4).
- Step back with the right foot (count 1).
- Brush the left foot to the right foot (count 2).
- Step to the side with the left foot (count 3).
- Close the right foot to the left foot (count 4).

Queens of Heart (Girls)
- Step back with the right foot (count 1).
- Brush the left foot to the right foot (count 2).
- Step to the side with the left foot (count 3).
- Close the right foot to the left foot (count 4).
- Step forward with the left foot (count 1).
- Brush right foot to the left foot (count 2).
- Step to the side with the right foot (count 3).
- Close the left foot to the right foot (count 4).

Funky, Futterwacken Freestyle

The showstopper, however, is Mad Hatter when he does a Futterwacken freestyle dance! He becomes the life of the party!

With a freestyle dance, you are free to express yourself and do whatever feels natural to you. In other words, there's no right or wrong way to dance freestyle. So go ahead, try some funky moves! Having fun is what a Futterwacken freestyle is all about.

Big Ben

London Bridge

Good Deeds Express

Buckingham Palace

Ready for the Queen!

With the life skills you've learned, you are ready for new and exciting adventures!

By understanding the winsome behavior and the Wonder-rules of the land, you will know how to act in all kinds of ways:

- You understand why it's important to seek knowledge and follow rules in order to be safe and have the most fun, just like Absolem.
- You can stand tall like Alice and introduce yourself confidently using your first and last name.
- You can use your best tea manners to honor your host and special guests, such as Alice.
- You can show curiosity and integrity as a host, like the Mad Hatter.
- You can be a delightful dream guest and show compassion, like Dormouse.
- You can give and receive gifts with humility, just like Cheshire Cat.
- You understand the importance of resilience and treating others with respect as well as showing respect for yourself, just like Tweedledee and Tweedledum.
- You can be kind and patient—never mean like the Red Queen!
- You can show creativity and gratitude with signature works of art, just like March Hare.
- When the occasion arises, you can even put your best foot forward with a basic box step and move as gracefully as the White Queen—or dance as silly as Mad Hatter!

"Perseverance = Success"

The EWF Motto

"Do well by doing good deeds."

EWF Core Values

Agility—Keeping your mind and body healthy and fit.

Compassion—Being kind and showing you care about others.

Confidence—Being sure of yourself and your skills.

Determination—Doing something and not giving up, even if it's difficult.

Dignity—Having respect for yourself.

Enthusiasm—Being cheerful and always looking for the best in others and every situation.

Graciousness—Being charming and doing nice gestures or good deeds.

Gratitude—Being thankful and feeling blessed.

Honor—Giving special care and attention to something or someone.

Humility—Being self-confident without bragging or boasting.

Knowledge—Becoming educated and learning valuable lessons and skills.

Obedience—Respecting and following the rules.

Patience—Learning to wait for something or someone without complaining.

Poise—Holding your head up and your shoulders back when sitting and standing.

Respect—How you feel about someone or how you treat someone.

Sincerity—Telling the truth and showing your true feelings.

Understanding—Accepting that others have beliefs or opinions different from your own.

"Teany" Bit of History

Afternoon Tea for Children

The tea custom is an enchanting ritual that dates back to ancient Chinese culture. It became popular in England by the early 1800s. What began as a light snack between meals to satisfy hunger evolved into an elaborate ritual. Today, teas are a wonderful way to spend time with friends and frolic in the afternoon.

Many hotels and tearooms serve afternoon tea and have a special menu just for children. Traditionally, tea is offered from two until five o'clock. Afternoon tea is served with fancy teapots and china cups. Kids usually have a choice of hot cocoa, lemonade, or tea. Finger sandwiches, scones, cupcakes, and cookies arrive at the table on tiered cake stands.

Teatime usually means that girls and boys get to play dress-up. Girls may go all out and wear fancy dresses with oversized hats or ornate headbands, whereas boys often choose button-down or collared shirts with khakis or trousers. For a more sophisticated look, boys may add a bowtie and blazer to an ensemble.

And one final note: the gesture of extending a pinky finger as you sip tea is really just an affectation and it's unnecessary! Teas should be fun, not stuffy.

Glossary

affectation—An exaggeration of something.

blini—A thin, tiny pancake often topped with various fillings.

crudités—The French word for bite-sized raw vegetables eaten as a finger food or a hors d'oeuvre.

canapés—The French word for little crackers, miniature toasts, or pastries.

Golden Deed—Doing a chore or being responsible for something without being reminded, such as putting your toys and games away or brushing your teeth after a meal.

Golden Rule—Treat others as you would want them to treat you, or "Do unto others as you would have them do unto you."

good deed—Doing something the first time you are asked to do it, such as your homework or going to bed.

Great Britain—Europe's largest island. It includes England, Scotland, and Wales.

manners—The civilized ways we treat others and perform tasks.

royal—Of notable excellence or magnificence; splendid.

rule—A guide for expected conduct or action.

winsome—To be charming and cheerful in a childlike way.

Magical Phrases and Words

The following words are magical and have special power. Use them often.

Please—Use this word when asking someone for something.

Thank you—This phrase is a polite way to accept a gift, compliment, or kind gesture.

You're welcome—This is a nice way to answer someone who says, "Thank you." It means you were happy to do a favor or kind gesture for them.

Excuse me—Say this phrase when you need to make an apology for something or when you need to get around someone.

I'm sorry—Saying this is a way to express either regret or sympathy.

EW Foundation Certificate of Achievement

"Do well by doing good deeds."

My Pledge

I pledge to do my best, exhibit gracious manners, and live by the Golden Rule.

_____

Child's Signature   Date

Quotes of Inspiration

"Those who bring sunshine to the lives of others cannot keep it from themselves."
—*Sir James M. Barrie, creator of Peter Pan*

"True happiness comes from the joy of deeds well done, the zest of creating things new."
—*Antoine de Saint-Exupéry*

"So shines a good deed in a weary world."
—*William Shakespeare and Willy Wonka*

"Go confidently in the direction of your dreams."
—*Henry David Thoreau*

"If you can dream it, you can do it."
—*Walt Disney*

About the EW Foundation

The EW Foundation (EWF) was founded in 2012 by Loretta Neff as a philanthropic organization that promotes the importance of character education and literacy programs through various charities, missions, and schools.

The EWF believes every child and young adult should receive an education that includes a strong social foundation. Through philanthropy, which plays a meaningful role in our organization, we hope to greatly enrich the lives of others with our care, commitment, and resources.

Mission

Our mission is to provide educational programs, financial resources, and volunteer support for the benefit of children and youth.

Vision

Our vision is to empower children and young adults with the social tools necessary to succeed in school and beyond; to provide value to our charity and school partners; and to improve the human condition worldwide.

The EW Foundation, a 501(c)(3) official nonprofit
561.833.0131
www.EWFcares.org
www.sipteawithmadhatter.com

All net proceeds from this book go to charity.

Honor Roll of Donors—EW FOUNDATION®

FOUNDERS SOCIETY
$10,000 to $24,999

S. Daniel Abraham
Arthur E. Benjamin
Richard McCready
Loretta A. Neff
Laurie A. Rumbaugh Family
Foundation
TD Wealth

LEGACY SOCIETY
$5,000 to $9,999

Connie M. Frankino Foundation
Dean and Raymer Maguire, III
Herme de Wyman Miro
Cheryl and Mark Montgomery
The International Society of Palm
Beach

CORPORATE SOCIETY
$2,000 to $4,999

Laina and Gregory D. Albert
BMO Private Bank
Suzanne Holmes
Patty Myura
Eleanor Patterson Reeves
Foundation

COMMUNITY ENRICHMENT
SOCIETY
$1,000 to $1,999

Josephine Linder duPont Bayard
BreakThru Beverage
Bill Horneck
Gail Kleinert
Brandy J. Lowe
La Casa Hermosa of Wellington

Jan and Chip Malley
MindsiCorp
Meaghan and Robert Pick
Provident Jewelry
Roberta Roller Rabbit
Jean and Daniel Schroeder
Kathy and Paul Sheridan
Rona and Gary Sterling
Grace and Richard Tissiere

MENTOR SOCIETY
$500 to $999 or In-Kind Donation

Carolyn Broadhead Sasso
Peter Björklund
Cristina Ciolacu
Beth Glass
Carol Jaeger
Nadine and David Fite
K is for Kids Foundation
Joanie Kamin
Elissa Kurland
MontBlanc
JoAnna Myers
Melissa Parker
Daniella Ortiz
The Emily Post Institute
Lizzie Post
Diane Sandler
Sally and Dominic Taglialatella
Vosges Haut-Chocolat
Gail Worth

AMBASSADOR SOCIETY
$100 to $499

Danielle Ball
The Braver Foundation
David Blanken
Louise Braver

Anne-Marie Campbell
Sharon and Ray Carnahan
Amy Collins
Dale Connor
Shani Core
Samantha Curry
Elayne Flamm
The David Foundation
Summer Foley
Vicki Foley
Barbara Friedman
Sharon Jablin
Nenita Go
Denise Gold
Gerald Goldsmith
Sara Griffen
Robin Groves
Picnic Fashion
Ginger Feuer
Suzi Goldsmith
Dr. and Mrs. Sheldon Guttman
Jeannie Kligman
Gertrude B. Nielsen Charitable
Trust
Jeri Meltzer
Dr. Brent Prather
Cari Rentas
Susan and Stuart Sakosits
Amanda Shumaker
Dr. Bonnie Sloan*
Mimi Vaughan
Elfriede Welch
Lena Yarina
Jennifer Ziegler
In memory of Randy Carnahan
In memory of Marlene Leininger
In memory of Karen Stack

About the Author

Loretta Neff is an award-winning children's book author and the founder of the EW Foundation®, a nonprofit provider of character education programs. Loretta has specialized in character and etiquette education since 1994 with clients ranging from children to Fortune 500 companies.

Loretta's books are inspired by her love of humanity and desire to share her resources with children who need them most. Through her books and charitable efforts, she hopes to engage young minds and instill the values that can shape and transform their lives in a meaningful and measurable way.

Her first book, award-winning *Tame Your Manners*, released March 2014, received coveted reviews and has become a bestseller in its genre. Described as "*Madagascar* meets manners," the book continues to charm the hearts of critics and readers alike.

Her second book, *Sip Tea with Mad Hatter*, is another delightful concept for introducing children to good character and tea manners. The book was inspired by *Alice in Wonderland* and will challenge kids to be creative and "Think outside the rabbit hole."

Based on EW Foundation's KAMP® curriculum, a 2015 and 2016 Promising Practices national award winner, her books emphasize good character and core values while offering an affordable and comprehensive learning solution. Children can enjoy the series at their own pace or share it as a family or class. (For ages 5–12.)

Loretta received a BA degree in 1989 with honors and had her sights on the legal profession. But after being accepted to law school at Michigan State University, she never attended, having found her real passion for philanthropic work and the teaching of business and social etiquette.

Loretta remains committed to the advancement of numerous charities, societies, and educational foundations.

Loretta is devoted to family, children's causes, and divides her time between Florida and Ohio.